PEMBROKESHIRE Profile

First in a Series

Edited by Miles Cowsill

Introduction 2
Foreword 4
The Story of Pembrokeshire 7
A Geographical Ramble 20
The Wildside of Pembrokeshire 29
Pembrokeshire Coast National Park 47
South Pembrokeshire 51
North Pembrokeshire 63
Acknowledgments 83
Map of Pembrokeshire 84

Sponsored by

**National Power
(PEMBROKE)**

Published by

Haven PUBLICATION PRODUCTIONS CYNHYRCHIADAU CYHOEDDI HAFAN

ISBN 0 9517627 0 6

INTRODUCTION

Pembrokeshire is an area of outstanding beauty with a variety of scenery in every corner of the county. The wild tall cliffs of the rugged coast and Presely Hills offer wonderful walks, a variety of wildlife and natural history. The golden sands, estuaries and wooded valleys combine to offer a land of magic and enchantment steeped in a fascinating history.

The former county of Pembrokeshire with its towering castles and ancient burial chambers form just part of the fascinating heritage of historical sites. The area boasts a wealth of outstanding parish churches and chapels set in countryside and coastal positions, where you least expect them.

The wild and vast Presely Hills dominate the county on a clear day. The views from the hills take in the dramatic coast and islands in the distance, which are continually at the mercy of the Atlantic seas. This breathtaking scenery is the home of rich and varied wildlife. The remote islands, free from the 20th century influence and the motor car, are the natural sanctuaries for probably some of the best reserves in the British Isles. To protect this special habitat, part of the region comes under the control for planning and protection of the Pembrokeshire Coast National Park Authority.

The beautiful coast, environment and the mild climate has made Pembrokeshire a favoured location for tourists over the decades. Tourism continues to grow as a result of Pembrokeshire becoming more accessible during the last twenty years, with the extension of the M4 and A48/A40.

Pembrokeshire not only relies on tourism but also agriculture, shipping and refining of oil from all over the world. Oil is very important to the local economy and this industry has had to work around and with the outstanding environment. The famous Pembrokeshire potato is still an important cash crop for farmers, as are dairy and sheep.

During the Seventies the Government reorganised the

A typical Tuesday morning scene at Haverfordwest mart, with farmers trying to 'eye up' the bargains. (Mark Richards)

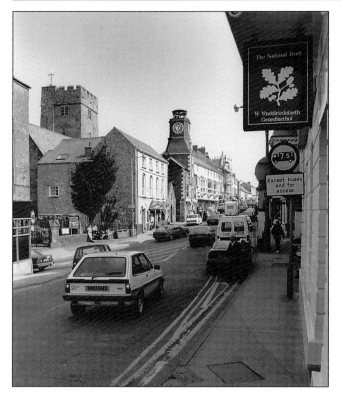

Looking up the busy Main Street of Pembroke. The town boasts two parish churches, both of the 13th century origin. (Miles Cowsill)

Presely Hills in the spring. (Miles Cowsill)

old counties of Wales into eight principal administration areas. As a result the new County of Dyfed was created out of three long established counties of West Wales: Pembrokeshire, Cardiganshire and Carmarthenshire. The town of Carmarthen was to become the new county town, and as a result Haverfordwest has lost some of its importance, nevertheless the town still retains a feel and air that all county towns seem to have in the British Isles. The former county boundaries of Pembrokeshire are now divided into two Local Authority areas, Preseli Pembrokeshire District Council and South Pembrokeshire District Council.

Despite the changes of the last twenty years, the wonderful heritage, charm and character of the region with its outstanding coastline and beautiful hinterland, have altered very little. With future commercial developments and the growth of tourism in the Nineties, Pembrokeshire I am sure will continue to offer that special feel which has attracted so many.

Miles Cowsill
Kilgetty, Pembrokeshire

FOREWORD

We at National Power's Pembroke Power Station are delighted to have the privilege of supporting this excellent book, which will enthrall holiday visitors and residents, with its top quality photographs which captures the essence of the old county. We are fortunate to be surrounded by such scenery and we are proud that our architects achieved the objective of reducing our impact on this special countryside

In the 1990's, leading to the 21st century, we are seeing the environment as one of the major issues in politics, culture and economics, affecting many developments in power, energy demands and standards of living.

It is all the more encouraging that when Pembroke Power Station was planned and built in 1965-70, the Central Electricity Generating Board took great care in its choice of design and exact location of the principal building to take account of the local environment and the proximity of the Pembrokeshire Coast National Park and the Milford Haven Waterway.

During World War II, the Milford Haven Waterway was an important naval and flying boat base but as these activities declined in importance after the war, so it was realised that there was an ever increasing demand for petroleum products and for ever growing tankers to carry this merchandise. When the Very Large Crude Carriers (V.L.C.C.) were being developed to a displacement of 250,000 tons it was not surprising that they found the long deep waters of Milford Haven an ideal anchorage from which to discharge their cargo.

By early 70's Esso, Texaco, Gulf and Amoco had built refineries on the shores of Milford Haven, and BP had built a pumping station to connect them to their Llandarcy Refinery.

One of the products of a refinery is residual oil, or heavy fuel oil, after all the higher fractions have been extracted from the crude oil, and it was logical to build a power station in the Milford Haven area to take advantage of the presence of the refineries and their products.

Every effort was made by C.E.G.B. to take full account of the impact of new power station upon the local environment. In the case of Milford Haven, with the Pembrokeshire Coast National Park and many popular holiday beaches in the near vicinity, it was even more important to minimise the impact of a power station upon its surroundings.

To this end the Board searched the area around the Haven until it nominated this location, the head of a drowned valley, as the most suitable site on which to build.

During the construction of the Power Station, a dam was built across the inlet so that the area could be drained, then the soil was excavated and removed so that the foundations could be dug from the bed rock. This had the effect of lowering the Station by some 30 feet, and the lowest floor is 32 feet below sea level.

This gave the Station a good measure of natural concealment as the valley sides obscure the buildings from most aspects except through the entrance to the Pembroke River, known as Pennar Gut.

When the buildings had been erected, the excavated soil was returned to the site from which it had been removed and this was laid and levelled to transform the drowned valley into a flat parkland around the Station.

The levelled basin with the natural framing of the valley sides, coupled with the careful selection of building materials and colours and intensive planting of trees and shrubs has transformed the site which now presents a highly acceptable aspect.

Only the 700 foot chimney can be seen from every side and for any distance and this was chosen to carry the exhaust gases high into the atmosphere to again minimise the Station's impact on the local environment.

A modern power station needs large quantities of water for cooling purposes, a readily accessible supply of fuel, a convenient connection to the national power distribution network or Grid, and a plentiful source of manpower.

The Pembroke site has proved to be ideal. The Haven readily allows the 4 huge circulating water pumps to extract up to 1 million gallons of water each minute, to be returned to the Haven a few minutes later and up to 8° celsius warmer.

The proximity of the refineries enables the Station to receive fuel from two pipelines, one across the bed of the Haven, and the fuel is stored in six large oil tanks hidden below the brow of the hill to the north of the site.

The power subsequently generated is readily transported by the grid to South Wales and on to the other side of the Severn Estuary north of Bristol.

The Station has employed up to 585 permanent workers but has gradually contracted over the years to a regular workforce of about 300, consisting of 60 engineers, 20 administrative and clerical staff, and 220 industrial staff.

The principal building on the site is the Turbine Hall, which is nearly 90 feet high and almost 1000 feet long. Here are installed the four turbo generators, each capable of supplying 500,000 single electric fires simultaneously. The total output of the Station is therefore equal to 2 million electric fires, or 2000 megawatts.

When the Station was designed it was envisaged that heavy fuel oil at £8 per tonne, rising to £15, would be comfortably cheaper than coal, but inflation and three Middle East wars have combined to drive oil prices up to £60 – £70 per tonne, rather higher than World coal prices.

As a consequence the generation of the Station fell from base load, i.e. 24 hour operation, to Peak Lopping, which requires coming onto load at times of peak demand and running for perhaps only a few hours in the morning and in the evening.

The Station is open to general members of the public on Tuesday, Wednesday and Thursday afternoons for the large number of visitors in the area from June to September. This permits visitors to view the whole generating process in clean conditions and in a relatively quiet atmosphere.

Pembroke Power Station. (National Power)

We confidently expect Pembroke Power Station to be generating well into the 2000's and believe we will have an increasingly important role to play as a young and very efficient large station.

Readers may be assured that we will spare no expense to ensure that our impact upon the surrounding countryside continues to be minimal.

D. Jackson
Station Manager, Pembroke

The church at Cwmyreglwys was destroyed in the Great Storm of 1859. (Miles Cowsill)

THE STORY OF PEMBROKESHIRE

When man first set foot on the remote peninsula that was to become Pembrokeshire the peninsula itself looked rather different. There was no St Bride's Bay, and the offshore islands of Ramsey and Skomer were protruding headlands guarding a coastal plain. Northward lay the land of the Lowland Hundred, now drowned under Cardigan Bay, and to the south one could walk from Caldey to Combe Martin on the Devon coast.

The first men came, during the Old Stone Age, in pursuit of their prey as it followed the retreating ice, and sought shelter in caves such as Hoyle's Mouth, near Tenby, and Priory Farm Cave at Monkton. They kindled fires in the cave entrance as a protection against the weather and wild beasts and left animal bones and flint tools as evidence of their presence.

When the weather grew less severe, some ten thousand years ago, there came a people that had developed a new technique in making small flint implements that could be used, for example, as arrow-heads or harpoon-barbs. They belonged to the Middle Stone Age and while some of them continued to live in caves, like Nanna's Cave on Caldey, others settled on coastal sites, within reach of the sea for fishing and for raw material in the shape of flint pebbles. Among the discarded tools and debris of a community living on Nab Head there was a new implement in the form of an elongated pebble that was used for knocking limpets off the rocks.

The sea continued to rise, as the ice melted, to give shape to the present coastline. Low tides at Amroth and Newgale reveal stumps of trees of submerged forests, and a flint point of an arrow found among the bones of a wild pig at Lydstep betokened a kill its Mesolithic hunter failed to retrieve. Memories of lost lands survive in legend, and by those who may see the Green Isles of Enchantment out at sea on magic moonlit nights.

Somewhere around 3000 BC the first farmers arrived.

They came by sea, hugging the coasts in their frail curragh-type craft, and settled where their corn was sown, to await its ripening, surrounded by their domesticated animals. Only one of their settlements has been found in Pembrokeshire, with traces of a small round structure and a rectangular building beneath the fortifications of a later hill-fort at Clegyr Boia, west of St. David's, and it is considered that the occupants concentrated on cattle raising as the site, and the climate, may have been unsuitable for growing corn. They are remembered, however, by the most remarkable great stone, or megalithic, monuments in the form of communal tombs or burial chambers. The chamber, or *cromlech,* was constructed by placing a massive capstone on upright stone pillars and covering the whole with stones or earth in the shape of a round, or long, mound. In most cases the mound has been removed by the elements or the hand of man leaving the naked stones which were fancifully taken to have been druids' altars or to have been raised by Samson with his little finger, as Carreg Samson, or 'quoits' thrown by King Arthur, as Carreg Goetan Arthur, or some other king, as King's Quoit at Manorbier. Pentre Ifan is one of the most spectacular chamber tombs in the country, with its curved facade and portal reminiscent of the portal dolmens of Ireland. These Neolithic, or New Stone Age, colonisers had previously settled along the Irish coast before coming here.

Forests had to be cleared to make cultivation possible and tree felling was effectively carried out with sharp-edged, polished stone axes, some of them made of spotted dolerite, or preselite, from outcrops at the eastern end of the Presely Hills, where there appears to have been an axe-factory producing axes of such quality that they were in demand as far afield as Antrim and Salisbury Plain.

The same spotted dolerite was used to make battle axes by men of the early Bronze Age who came bearing metal that was yet too scarce or precious to use in making heavy implements. These were the Beaker Folk,

The crags of Carn Menyn, a source of the 'bluestones' of Stonehenge. (Miles Cowsill)

so called from the shapely drinking vessels which they buried as grave goods with their dead under pudding-shaped mounds, or barrows. The preponderance of barrows along the upland route on the Presely Hills, and the Ridgeway in the south, indicates that not all those who travelled these routes from Wessex to Ireland to bring back gold from Wicklow Hills were able to complete the journey.

The Presely Hills were of special significance, or even sanctity, to the people of this period and the dolerites and other stones, generally referred to as 'bluestones', may well have been symbolic of the veneration. For some reason men were sufficiently motivated to perform an act unparalleled in the prehistory of the western world by transporting more than eighty stone pillars all the way to Salisbury Plain eventually to become part of the great monument of Stonehenge. The stones, conveniently split into shape by natural fraction and weathering, were taken from Carnmenyn and surrounding igneous outcrops and hauled overland to **Canaston Bridge** to be floated down Milford Haven and

up the Bristol Channel and the Bristol Avon and the Frome until they had to be taken overland again to the Wylye, and then up the Hampshire Avon. The Altar Stone, and another stone now lost, came from the shores of Milford Haven, perhaps in place of lost or damaged bluestones. A spotted dolerite boulder found in Boles Barrow at Heytesbury may also have been discarded on the way and, if that is the case, it shows that the bluestones were transported to Wessex centuries before they were erected at Stonehenge.

Gors Fawr is a tiny thing compared with Stonehenge. It is the only stone circle in Pembrokeshire, its sixteen boulders forming an egg-shaped ring, standing on a purple moor within sight of the source of the bluestones. Meini Gŵyr is the only embanked circle in Wales.

Most common of the megalithic monuments in Pembrokeshire are the standing stones, and at the same time, the most mysterious. They appear to have formed part of complex Bronze Age ritual practices that are not yet understood. They are sometimes to be seen in pairs, as at Cerrig Meibion Arthur, and at Parc-y-meirw there is a rare alignment of eight stones, now mostly concealed in hedgebanks.

Bronze gave way to iron with the arrival of groups of

Stonehenge is located on the vastness of the Salisbury Plain in Wiltshire. Presely 'bluestones' form the inner circle. (Linda Cowsill)

A replica Iron Age round house at Castell Henllys.
(Miles Cowsill)

warlike Celts in about 500 BC. Their fortified settlements are scattered all over Pembrokeshire. Tall promontories that thrust out into the sea have defensive banks built across the neck to protect them from landward. The promontory fort on St. David's Head has the formidable Warriors' Dyke for its defence. The Deer Park is the largest promontory fort in Wales. Inland there are many hill-top settlements enclosed by ramparts and among them three great hill-forts: Moel Drygarn, Carn Ingli and Garn Fawr, each with the visible remains of hut platforms and enclosures that provided refuge for women, children and stock in the event of enemy attack. Traces of Iron Age fields are to be seen on the slopes above Porth Melgan and on Skomer Island, which has one of the best preserved ancient field systems in Wales.

The Celts brought with them a new culture and a language that survives, in one of its derivative forms, as the Welsh language.

The Roman legions kept clear of Pembrokeshire. They came as far as Carmarthen, which became a defended Roman settlement, with an amphitheatre to seat up to five thousand people. Apart form Roman finds, mostly coins, their only traces are the Romanised farmsteads at Castle Flemish and Trelissey The claim that a Roman road, the Via Julia, ran westward from Carmarthen to St.

David's arose from an eighteenth century forgery, and the Emperor Magnus Maximus's hunting expedition on Y Freni Fawr has no historical foundation.

Late in the fourth century an Irish tribe, the Deisi, from Co. Meath in Ireland, migrated to Pembrokeshire under their leader, Eochaid Allmuir, and established a royal dynasty that was to rule in south-west Wales for some five centuries. They provided the first written records in the form of inscribed stones bearing the names of those who were considered worthy of commemoration. The writing was in Latin or in ogham, an Irish alphabet designed for ease of cutting on the edge of a stone pillar. Many of these stones have been rescued and placed in churches or churchyards for safe keeping, as at Brawdy, Mathry, Maenclochog and Cilgerran. A stone in St Dogmael's church, used in decoding the ogham alphabet, has in Latin *Sagarani fili Cunotami* with the ogham *Sagrani maqi Cunatami,* commemorating one Sagranus son of Cunotamus. The Goidelic *maqi,* from which 'mac' derives, would have been *map* or *ap* if Sagranus had been a Welshman.

The inscriptions date from fifth century onward, by which time Christianity had been long established here. Pembrokeshire lay on the route of the Celtic saints, as the early missionaries were known, who travelled between Ireland and Rome or Jerusalem. It also had its own saint, David, born at St. David's to St Non, who is remembered by a chapel and a well above St Non's Bay. David was so revered that close on sixty churches have been dedicated to him in south-west Wales, together with eight in Cornwall and seven more in Brittany. His shrine became a place of pilgrimage to the extent that two visits to St. David's equalled one to Rome.

Work on the cathedral church was begun by Bishop Peter de Leia in 1178, and later bishops have added to the original edifice. Bishop Henry Gower gave the Bishop's Palace its arcaded parapet and grand proportions, and St Mary's College was founded by Bishop Adam Houghton.

A slab in the wall of the south transept commemorates

The towering castle of Haverfordwest is located in the centre of the town. During the 18th and 19th century the castle was used as a jail and later became a police station. Today it houses a museum. (Miles Cowsill)

Hedd and Isaac, the sons of Bishop Abraham who was slain by the Norsemen, bands of whom marauded the Pembrokeshire coasts from the middle of the ninth century onward and plundered the cathedral on eight or more occasions. They left only their names on the offshore islands and on a few coastal settlements, like Angle and Goultrop and Dale in the south, and Fishguard in the north.

The Normans lost no time in invading south Wales once its powerful prince, Rhys ap Tewdwr, was killed in 1093. Roger de Montgomery, Earl of Shrewsbury, and his son, Arnulf, swept across Wales to Pembroke and there 'a slender fortress built of stakes and turf'. Arnulf later joined his brother, Robert, in revolt against the king, Henry I, and was banished, and Pembroke became a royal lordship with Gerald de Windsor as its custodian. Gerald married Nest, the daughter of Rhys ap Tewdwr, the 'Helen of Wales', and their sons, the FitzGeralds, were prominent in the invasion of Ireland, and in its Anglo-Norman settlement. Their grandson, Giraldus Cambrensis, born at Manorbier in 1146, accompanied Archbishop Baldwin of Canterbury on his tour of Wales, preaching the Third Crusade, and was dispatched by Henry II to Ireland as escort for Prince, later King, John, and wrote perceptive accounts of both countries.

In north Pembrokeshire Robert FitzMartin occupied the Welsh stronghold at Nevern and established a Norman lordship in the hundred of Cemais. The hundred of Pebidiog, in which St. David's lay, remained in the hands of the bishop, but the Welsh bishop was replaced by a Norman.

Nowhere in Wales was the Anglo-Norman grip stronger than in south Pembrokeshire. A line of powerful castles reaching from Roch to Tenby was supported by a string of lesser fortresses along the foothills of the Presely Hills. In addition, there were the great castles of Carew, Manorbier and Pembroke, the impressive donjon which was built by William Marshal, who succeeded as Earl of Pembroke in 1199.

The Normans did not come alone; they brought large

numbers of English followers whose anglicising influence was such that the southern part of Pembrokeshire became known a 'Little England beyond Wales'. There was also an infusion of Flemings, sent by Henry I, who were, Giraldus states, 'very hostile to the Welsh and in perpetual state of conflict with them.'

The Welsh harassed the Anglo-Normans from the outset, and regained their territories except for Pembroke Castle. In 1096 they laid siege to the castle but they were hoodwinked by Gerald de Windsor who, although he had hardly any provisions left, threw his last few flitches of bacon over the palisade at the besiegers to make them believe that he was well supplied. The Welsh withdrew but only to fight and fight again, against overwhelming odds. Rhys ap Gruffydd recovered south

Roch Castle situated on its rocky perch overlooking the countryside. (Miles Cowsill)

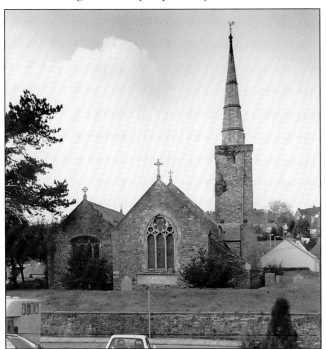

The pretty church of St.Martin's boasts to be the oldest church in Haverfordwest. In recent years the church has been greatly restored. (Miles Cowsill)

Pembrokeshire in 1189, and Llywelyn the Great came in 1215, and Llywelyn the Last in 1257 overran the Norman lordships, but Pembroke was never taken.

A contingent of French mercenaries landed in Milford Haven in August 1405 to assist Owain Glyndwr in his rising. They marched on Haverfordwest, which they occupied apart from its castle, before proceeding to take Carmarthen.

On 28 January 1457, at Pembroke Castle, the thirteen year old Margaret Beaufort, Lancastrian heiress to the throne, gave birth to a son, Henry Tudor. Her husband, Edmund Tudor, Earl of Richmond, had died at Carmarthen the previous year and had been buried in the Greyfriars, the house of the Franciscan Friars, but at the dissolution of the monasteries the tomb was removed to St. David's Cathedral. In 1471, young Henry had to flee from the Yorkists with his uncle Jasper Tudor, Earl of Pembroke: they sailed from Tenby and landed in Brittany and another fourteen years were to pass before he returned.

On Sunday evening, 7 August 1485, just before sundown Henry landed at Mill Bay on the Dale peninsula, and, early next morning, marched through Haverfordwest and set off on the long journey to Bosworth Field where he defeated Richard III and became King Henry VII, founder of the Tudor dynasty.

Among those who had helped him was Rhys ap Thomas, the most influential magnate in west Wales, who had been able to raise 'a great bande of soldiers'. He had marched his men from Carmarthen through mid-Wales to join Henry's army and Welsh contingents from the north at Long Mountain, near Welshpool. After the battle, Rhys was made chamberlain of south Wales and, in 1505, he was appointed Knight of the Garter, an honour which he celebrated with a magnificent tournament at Carew Castle.

Henry VIII abolished the county palatine that had existed since Gilbert de Clare had been created the first Earl of Pembroke in 1138, and united it with the several other lordships to form the county of Pembroke as one of the thirteen counties of Wales. He appointed Anne Boleyn Marchioness of Pembroke, and through her influence William Barlow was made Prior of the Augustinian Priory at Haverfordwest and, soon after, Bishop of St. David's. Barlow became the king's chief instrument in carrying through the religious changes following the Reformation, and the diocese of St. David's led the way in promoting Protestantism, at the same time acting as a buffer against the invasion of Popish influences from Ireland. Barlow set out to suppress pilgrimages to the shrine of the patron saint and endeavoured to remove the see from such 'a barbarous and desolate corner', but succeeded only in dismantling the Bishop's Palace and establishing the episcopal residence at Abergwili near Carmarthen.

The restoration of the old religion with the accession of Mary in 1553 brought only three martyrdoms in Wales, two of whom had Pembrokeshire connections. Robert Ferrar, Bishop of St. David's, was burned at the stake at Carmarthen, and William Nichol, who is otherwise unknown, suffered the same fate in High Street, Haverfordwest, on 9 April 1558.

The greater part of the monastic property, following the dissolution of the monasteries, came into the hands of the landed families among whom the bishop's brothers, Thomas and Roger Barlow, acquired the lands of the Commandery of the Knights of St John of Jerusalem at Slebech, of the Priory of Pill and of the houses of the Augustinians and Black Friars at Haverfordwest.

The most powerful man in Pembrokeshire in the sixteenth century was Sir John Perrot, reputedly the natural son of Henry VIII by Mary Berkeley, a royal lady-in-waiting and wife of Sir Thomas Perrot of Haroldston. He was three times mayor of Haverfordwest and was the town's greatest benefactor. He was appointed President of Munster and Lord Deputy of Ireland. He enlarged Carew Castle, which he had been granted but was unable to complete the work. He was charged with treason for having uttered disrespectful references to the Queen and sentenced to death, but died a natural death while confined to the Tower of London before the sentence could be carried out.

In north Pembrokeshire, George Owen of Henllys, lord of Cemais, is commemorated in Nevern church as the 'Patriarch of English Geologists', but he is better remembered as the author of *The Description of Penbrokshire* (1603) which provides an unrivalled contemporary account of life in his native county. Among other prominent Pembrokeshire Elizabethans were Thomas Phaer, who translated Virgil's *Aeneid* and made medical science intelligible in English, and Robert Recorde of Tenby, who is claimed to have introduced the equal sign in mathematics.

The rise of Puritanism created a demand for the Bible to be translated into Welsh. Dr William Salesbury undertook the translation of the New Testament in 1567 and was assisted by Richard Davies, Bishop of St. David's, and Thomas Huet, the Precentor, but before they had completed the Old Testament, they quarrelled, and Wales had to wait another twenty years before it had a Welsh Bible. Devotional works were also published in an effort to raise moral stands, outstanding among which was *Canwyll y Cymry* (The Welshmen's Candle) containing rhymes and verses that were easy to commit to memory and made religion available to the masses who could not afford, or read, the Bible. Its author, Rhys Prichard, 'the old Vicar', was Chancellor of St. David's Cathedral. The people of Pembrokeshire had pronounced Puritan sympathies, but the movement suffered because of the hostile attitude of the former Bishop of St. David's, William Laud, by now Archbishop of Canterbury.

George Fox, the founder of the Society of Friends, came to Pembroke and Haverfordwest in 1657 and, before long, there were Quaker meetings held at Redstone, near Narberth, Puncheston, St. David's, Newport, Jameston and Haverfordwest. By 1661 Lewis David of Llanddewi Velfrey and others were imprisoned for their beliefs and their persecution continued until they emigrated to Pennsylvania where David had purchased 3,000 acres of land from William Penn. There they settled in townships which they named Haverford and Narberth.

At the same time, Peregrine Phillips, vicar of Llangwm and Freystrop until he was ejected for failing to conform to the tenets of the established church, became the first pastor of the Green Meeting at Haverfordwest and made it the mother-church of Nonconformity in Pembrokeshire. The Baptists built their first chapel at Rhydwilym in 1668.

Another Pembrokeshire man, John Gambold of Purcheston, embraced the Moravian faith and was appointed their bishop with oversight of the brethren in Great Britain and Ireland. His brother, George Gambold, built a Moravian chapel on St Thomas's Green, Haverfordwest.

The Methodist Revival made an early impact on the county, partly due to the influence of Griffith Jones, rector of Llanddowror, who introduced his 'Circulating Schools' to provide education for young and old, and partly through the diligence of his curate, Howel Davies,

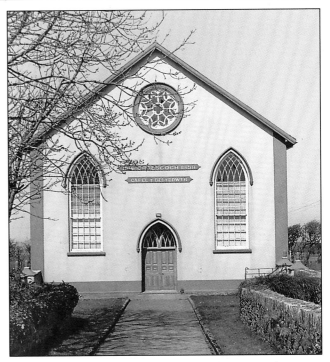

The Baptist Chapel at Croes-goch with its fine Gothic frontage in plasterwork. (Miles Cowsill)

'the Apostle of Pembrokeshire'. John Wesley visited Haverfordwest no less than fourteen times between 1763 and 1790, by when the landscape was dappled with chapels of various denominations.

North Pembrokeshire was for the king when the Civil War broke out in 1642, whereas the south supported Parliament. The royalist commander, the Earl of Carbery, advanced into the county in the summer of the following year and prepared to attack Pembroke, but found Major General Rowland Laugharne, the Parliamentary leader, and his troops, assisted by a Parliamentary fleet in Milford Haven, more than a match, and he had to retreat. Carbery was replaced by Sir Charles Gerard, a professional soldier, who quickly re-established royalist control, but on 1 August 1644 Laugharne routed the

The winter sun catches the cromlech at Pentre Ifan. (Brace Harvatt Associates)

St. Issell's Church set in an attractive wooded valley on the outskirts of the village of Saundersfoot. (Miles Cowsill)

The Baptist Chapel at Rhydwilym hidden in the valley by the side of a tumbling stream. The Chapel is reputed to be the oldest in Wales. (Miles Cowsill)

royalists at the battle of Colby Moor, between Wiston and Llawhaden. The royalists lost 150 men killed and 700 taken prisoner, as against the Parliament losses of two dead and sixty wounded.

The Second Civil War was precipitated in 1648 by the volte-face of the Parliamentary leaders. John Poyer, mayor, refused to surrender Pembroke to Colonel Fleming, who had been appointed governor, and injudiciously fired on Fleming's troops. Poyer and Laugharne held out at Pembroke, and Colonel Rice Powell, one of Laugharne's lieutenants, at Tenby. Cromwell decided on a show of strength and arrived to suppress 'the Welsh insolence', but Pembroke withstood a siege that lasted forty-eight days. Laugharne, Poyer and Powell were sentenced to death but it was decreed that only one should die. They refused to draw lots, and a small child handed them each a slip of paper, two of

which bore the words 'Life given by God': the other was blank. Poyer had the blank one and was shot by a firing squad at Covent Garden on 25 April 1649.

Charles Stuart, Prince of Wales, exiled in Jersey, was captivated by the 'brown, beautiful, bold but insipid' Lucy Walter, daughter of William Walter of Roch and Rosemarket. She became the mother of his eldest illegitimate son, James, Duke of Monmouth who, after the death of his father, landed at Lyme Regis and was proclaimed king by Protestant adherents at Taunton, but the battle of Sedgemoor sealed his fate. Lucy died in poverty in Paris in 1658.

The Pembrokeshire gentry remained loyal Jacobites and many of them were prominent members of the Society of Sea Serjeants that met at Tenby and other seaside towns in south-west Wales. They wore as a badge a silver dolphin within a roundel set on an eight-pointed silver star, which also decorated their glasses as they drank a toast to 'the little gentleman in black velvet', a reference to the mole that raised a molehill against which William IV's horse stumbled and fatally unseated its rider.

Welshmen in London supporting the Hanoverians formed the Most Honourable and Loyal Society of Ancient Britons, the treasurer of which was Sir Watkin Lewes, son of the rector of Meline and Newport, and Lord Mayor of London in 1700.

On the evening of 22 February 1797, a French force landed at Carreg Wastad Point on Strumble Head. It comprised 1,400 men, more than a half of whom were 'abandoned rogues' released from goals of France. Their commander was an elderly Irish American, Colonel William Tate, who established his headquarters at Trehowel Farm. His hungry troops fell to ransacking the well-stocked larders of the surrounding farmhouses, supplemented by a supply of wine obtained from the recent wreckage of a smuggler. The Pembroke Yeomanry and other available soldiery, totalling 750 men were assembled and marched from Haverfordwest under the command of Lord Cawdor, while the local peasantry stood by with their billhooks and scythes. Their women, who had gathered on the facing slopes at Fishguard in their red shawls, were taken by the French for 'troops for the line to the number of several thousand'. Tate surrendered and signed articles of capitulation at the farmhouse before being taken along byways to Haverfordwest, as he feared the fury of the people of Fishguard. His men piled their arms on Goodwick beach. The last invasion of Britain was over having lasted less than forty-eight hours.

The Pembroke Yeomanry was awarded the battle honour 'Fishguard' which it wears with pride as the only unit of the British Army to have been so honoured for facing the enemy on British soil. A monument in St Mary's churchyard at Fishguard commemorates Jemima Nicholas who brought in a dozen Frenchmen at the points of a pitchfork.

The French wars were followed by a period of poverty and rural discontent, and there was considerable agitation for parliamentary reform, a powerful advocate of which, through the medium of his weekly paper, *Seren Gomer* was Joseph Harries, a native of Wolfscastle.

The discontent reached a climax on the night of 13 May 1839 when a group of countrymen, dressed in women's clothing, tore down a toll gate that had been erected on the Cardigan to Narberth road at Efailwen. This was the first of many incidents that were known as the Rebecca Riots. The perpetrators were local farmers and smallholders who had to pay ever-heavier tolls to take their carts along the turnpike roads. They were otherwise law-abiding, chapel-going people, and they undoubtedly had in mind the incident in the book of Genesis where as she left home to become Isaac's wife, her family 'blessed Rebecca and said unto her: "Thou art our sister; be thou the mother of thousands of millions, and let thy seed possess the gates of those which hate them"'.

Agriculture has always been the main industry in Pembrokeshire. In addition to the traditional mixed farming, it has specialised, in the last half century, in early potatoes, turkey breeding and vegetables, notably cauliflower and broccoli, have been grown on a limited scale. There have been several attempts at growing flowers, particularly daffodils, and one grower, at least, is exporting bulbs to Holland.

The fishing industry brought prosperity to the town of Milford in the early part of this century, and made it one of the leading fishing ports in the kingdom. Founded in 1790 by Sir William Hamilton, and pronounced by Lord Nelson, along with Trincomalee, the finest harbour he had ever seen, Milford became, in turn, a station for Quaker whalers from Nantucket, a naval dockyard and an Irish steam packet terminal, but the demand for whale oil ceased, the Admiralty moved the dockyard to Pembroke Dock and the Irish boats went to Fishguard. As the fishing industry declined, Milford began to develop as an oil port.

By the end of the eighteenth century, Pembrokeshire had been discovered as a place of resort for holidays. Travellers to the continent were prevented from doing so by the French wars, and there were those who wished to benefit from the newly-found healing properties of sea water. At Tenby, the old fishermen's chapel on the pier was converted by Dr John Jones, 'apothecary of Haverfordwest', into a bathing-house and, soon after, Sir William Paxton provided more elegant premises with 'a spacious vestibule for servants to wait, without mixing with the company.' Other facilities followed so that, as a resort, it was 'unrivalled in the Principality'.

Professor J A Steers, the acknowledged authority on the coasts of Britain, held the view that 'no part of the coastline of England and Wales is more beautiful or more interesting than that of Pembrokeshire'. In February 1952, that coastline was designated the Pembrokeshire Coast National Park, which included also the upper reaches of the Daugleddau and the Presely Hills. The Pembrokeshire Coast National Park Authority has the difficult, often conflicting, task of protecting the Park from despoliation and, at the same time, making it available for the enjoyment of its residents and of those who come as visitors.

Dillwyn Miles

An impressive aerial view of St.Ann's Head at the entrance to the Haven. The coastguard station and lighthouse can be seen above the dramatic folding and faulting of the rocks. (John Evans)

A fine example of vertical bedding at Lydstep Headland. Caldey Island can be seen in the background. (Anna Sutcliffe)

PEMBROKESHIRE – A GEOGRAPHICAL RAMBLE

To try and understand Pembrokeshire, the visitor must first look over his shoulder at the distant past. The land is shaped the way it is by the nature of the underlying rocks and the way in which they are changed by the constant process of weathering. The fact that Pembrokeshire contains such a tremendous variety of rock types within a comparatively small area helps to create the sharp contrasts for which the county is renowned. From majestic cliffs to sand dunes, from broad river estuary to cascading stream, from gently rolling arable land to rocky outcrop – all are to be seen within a few miles of each other. It is this constantly changing scenery which gives Pembrokeshire its fascination and which gives rise to the blossoming tourist industry which it has so rightly earned itself.

Generally speaking, the oldest rocks lie in the north while the south is mainly composed of younger rocks. To quote complex Geological time scales will be quite meaningless to most readers who may find it difficult enough to comprehend even one hundred years. With some of the oldest rocks of the area thought to be in excess of 1000 million years old, the reader will appreciate that much has happened during that span of time. The fact that these rocks still exist indicates that they are immensely hard and that weathering (the breakdown of the rock) must occur very slowly. Writing this from my home in Kent, I am mindful of the fact that had Pembrokeshire been composed of the soft rocks with which this county abounds, then the relentless action of the Atlantic Ocean would by now have removed most of it.

Many of the rocky outcrops we see in Pembrokeshire are simply stumps – the foundations of impressive mountains and volcanoes which once covered parts of the region. As the elements have inevitably broken them down and reduced boulder to stone and stone to pebble, so the soils have been formed on which today's farmers strive to eke out their living.

A Pembrokeshire milestone dominated by a modern signpost. (Miles Cowsill)

The rocks roughly run from east to west and thus meet the angry Atlantic Ocean at right angles. The harder the rock so the slower the rate of break-down (erosion) and the further out into the sea it will stand. The reverse also applies – softer rocks erode faster and instead of forming headlands with plunging cliffs, they tend to form flatter landscapes and bays in which the sea may deposit sand or material removed from those nearby cliffs. Yesterday's cliffs are today's beaches by way of constant rolling, smashing, tumbling and reducing in size. The lighter and smaller the material, the easier it is for the sea to transport and deposit it. St. Bride's Bay, the largest bay in Pembrokeshire, lies between St. David's Head in the north and Wooltack Point in the south. Both headlands have adjacent offshore islands – Ramsey and Skomer – which before the sea created them were part of the headlands off which they now lie.

For approximately 300 days each year the wind blows from the south west piling up the sea and hurtling it against the coast which almost imperceptibly retreats under this onslaught. The sea picks up rocks and boulders and hurls them at the cliffs causing under-cutting and eventual collapse. Weaknesses are exploited, caves are formed and if two caves on either side of a headland join-up, back to back, an arch is formed. The splendid Green Bridge of Wales is an excellent example seen in the limestone cliffs of the Castlemartin peninsula, an area which is said by many to contain the finest section of such scenery in the British Isles.

When the arch collapses, as it inevitably will, a tall, isolated pinnacle of rock will remain and is called a stack. Stack Rocks (or the Elegug Stacks), close to the Green Bridge, are two of the many such features in Pembrokeshire.

Some of the caves in the area are extremely deep and air trapped inside them by surging seas will be compressed and forced into their roofs, causing shattering and collapse. Eventually a natural chimney may be formed which leads vertically to the cliff top above. The unsuspecting walker, beating his way along

The former slate quarries at Rosebush. This view takes in the reservoir and the Presely Hills. (John Hendy)

the coastal footpath in a stiff sou' wester, will have to be aware of these blow-holes. A sudden roaring, the shaking of the ground at his feet and a nearby eruption of wind-blown spray can be an unnerving experience for all but the strongest of heart!

Sometimes the complete cave roof can collapse after which a long, finger-inlet (or Geo) is formed. The best example of this is Huntsman's Leap, just west of St. Govan's Head, in the same area of limestone coastline.

But it is not only time and the sea which have moulded Pembrokeshire into the form we see today. The greatest force of all was ice.

During the last Ice Age, ice covered large areas of the British Isles. Although no ice sheets or glaciers now exist within these islands, the clues are still there for us to see. Imagine a bulldozer, some half mile high, being driven through the centre of your local town, across the fields, over the hills and into the sea. What devastation!

The ice sheet approached Pembrokeshire from the north west and, it slowly ground its way across the area smoothing out the features, flattening rocks, powdering boulders, hollowing out softer regions and carrying away all in its path. When at last the world's climate grew warmer (about 15,000 years ago), the ice began to melt and retreated northwards. The load which the ice sheet had carried along in front, inside and on top of it was simply dumped onto the land, with much of the lighter material being washed away by the vast amounts of water running off and through the melting ice. How do we know where the ice sheets came from? Scattered throughout the countryside are a series of 'alien' rocks. They are 'foreigners'. They don't belong and they sit there totally out of place. In the village of Bosherston lies such a stone – a glacial 'erratic' – which has its origins in Scotland while others came from the Isle of Man and the Hebridean islands. The ice sheet simply picked them up, carried them along and deposited them.

The melting ice caused the gradual raising of sea level and at this time, the Cleddau estuary was drowned forming the 24 mile long Milford Haven. This drowned

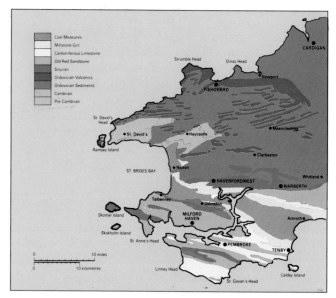

The Green Bridge of Wales. (John Hendy)

The Elegug Stacks are a favourite home for guillemots. (South Pembrokeshire District Council)

valley, seen on a smaller scale at Solva, is known as a 'ria'. Submerged forests – there are a number of them around the coast – are also pointers to the raising of the sea level.

So much water flowed from the melting ice sheets that new valleys were cut. The steep-sided Gwaun valley, east of Fishguard, is a well known example of a glacial spillway although recent research has suggested that it was formed by a flowing river *under* the melting ice. In other areas, we may be a little more certain. At Dinas Head, Dinas 'Island' is separated from the mainland by a narrow stretch of flat marshland which was once a glacial spillway. The Treffgarne Gorge (on the Haverfordwest – Fishguard road) is yet another fine example. When driving north through this spectacular feature, try to imagine a solid wall of water crashing down towards the Haven behind you. Pembrokeshire was certainly a very wet place up until about 12,000 years ago.

It is only right that the magnificent coastal scenery of

Tenby Railway Station in July 1983. The Inter-City 125 train has just arrived from Pembroke Dock en-route to Paddington. Meanwhile the Class 47 Diesel takes on passengers for Birmingham. (Miles Cowsill)

Pembrokeshire should be set apart and has, since 1952, been designated a National Park. Many visitors simply come to walk the 167 mile Long Distance Path (opened in 1971) and fail to explore the county's interior. To visit Pembrokeshire without visiting the Presely Hills is certainly a waste of a wonderful opportunity.

These ancient uplands are all that remains of a mountain range which was forced up by earth movements some 400 million years ago. From the heights of Foel-cwmcerwyn just east of Rosebush, on a clear day the most magnificent of all Pembrokeshire vistas can be seen. To the south is Milford Haven beyond which lies the Bristol Channel with Lundy Island and the Exmoor Hills of Devon dim blurrs in the sun. To the west it is possible to see the Wicklow Mountains in the Irish Republic while to the north, the wild peaks of Snowdonia can sometimes be observed. How fortunate is the visitor who is able to enjoy this complete panorama for sadly it is not a common sight.

Mention of Rosebush inevitably reminds us of the county's industrial past for tucked away behind the street lie the deserted remains of the four slate quarries. Here, heat and pressure baked the local shales forming a dark blue slate, which was in demand throughout the land – even on the roof of the Palace of Westminster. A railway was built up the valley from Clunderwen via Maenclochog and brave attempts were made to turn the hamlet of Rosebush into a holiday resort. Lakes were dug and stocked with fish, a hotel was built and advertisements proclaiming the resort's health-giving properties in 'the land of the Leek' were posted. Even though the line pushed on to Fishguard, the mighty Great Western Railway later abandoned it choosing to construct a railway which followed less tortuous terrain. One of the original locomotives from the Maenclochog Railway, *Margaret,* still survives as an exhibit in Scolton Manor Country Park while at Rosebush, its old engine shed stands roofless amidst the towering man-made mountains of slate. It is a truly evocative place. Other Victorian industries briefly thrived: granite, silver and lead, wool, fishing, iron and most importantly coal which represents some of the youngest solid rocks in Pembrokeshire.

The Pembrokeshire Coalfield was a part of the much larger South Wales Coalfield to the east across Carmarthen Bay. The coal seams, laid down about 320 million years ago when the area was a tropical swampland, run in a narrow band from Carmarthen Bay in the east to St. Bride's Bay in the west. Most of the early mines were drifts – tunnels in the sides of hills and valleys – and the coal is known to have been mined as long ago as Tudor times. As the reserves were dug out, so more dangerous and expensive methods were found to win it. Unfortunately the seams were faulted and thin and although the smokeless anthracite coal was highly sought after, the coming of a new order after Nationalisation of the Coal Industry in 1947, saw the final Pembrokeshire pits closed in the following year. The coal industry had made Saundersfoot, around which there were a number of pits, and from its tiny harbour much of the area's coal was exported. The coal seams can still be seen in the cliffs at Littlehaven and Broadhaven and adjacent to Saundersfoot. The deep cuttings through which the A 477 runs east of Kilgetty, also show the thin, contorted measures.

Pembroke Dock was a naval dockyard until 1926 and many famous ships were built there including the *Lion* which in 1847 was the largest vessel in the Royal Navy. During its later years, Pembroke Dock concentrated in the construction of destroyers and light cruisers and during the Second World War it came to life again with ship-repairing becoming its main activity.

The most important industry today is oil. The deep and sheltered waters of Milford Haven enable large tankers of up to 275,000 tons to use it. Since BP and Esso started operations during the 1950's, the Haven's fortunes have fluctuated. During the boom years of the 1970's, there were five oil terminals and four oil refineries in addition to the oil fired power station at Pembroke. The 62 mile pipeline to a refinery at

A view of the Haven with a Texaco tanker discharging at the Angle jetty. (Texaco)

Llandarcy (near Swansea) was built and much wealth was brought to the area. Sadly, recession set in and the operation has been scaled-down with Esso closing in 1984 and the BP terminal a year later. Future oil or gas finds in the Celtic Sea will undoubtedly revive the area's fortunes.

Pembrokeshire has a climate of its own. It is surrounded on three sides by the sea and the warming influence of the North Atlantic Drift keeps summers cool and winters mild. The overall range of temperatures is therefore slight and the coastal districts are usually spared frosts or snow. Rainfall however, increases with altitude. Tenby boasts some 40 inches each year while the Presely Mountains have half as much again. The region's exposed position makes it a very windy place and as a rule trees are not found near the exposed coasts. Those which do manage to survive the salty atmosphere and sea spray are usually twisted or stunted.

The mild climate allows a longer growing season. Springs are early, winters are rarely severe and so the potato growers of Pembrokeshire have the ideal

1. The Stena Felicity, *the largest ferry ever to operate from Fishguard, is captured here in the spring sun arriving from Rosslare.*
(Miles Cowsill)
2. *Until the Cleddau Bridge was opened 1975, car drivers wanting to reach the other side of the Haven had to take the ferry from Hobbs Point to Neyland or face a 16 mile drive around upper reaches of the Cleddau. Today, the bridge handles over 2 million cars each year, while Hobbs Point offers a pleasant resting point for car drivers to watch the shipping and pleasure boats on the Haven.*
(Miles Cowsill)
3. *Gulf Oil Refinery captured against the setting sun. (Gulf)*

The mighty winter storms pounding Strumble Head. (John Evans)

conditions and the county is famous for its early potatoes. In coastal areas, winter grown cereal crops are becoming more popular while inland, dairy and beef cattle thrive on the luxuriant pastures which the rain produces. Although soils are often deep, drainage is frequently poor and sheep can suffer from foot rot. The higher slopes where soils are thin and windswept, still see large areas occupied by sheep although life is difficult here and we still see a spring migration to the hills and a winter move back to the more sheltered valleys. Recent diversification has seen deer farming on the increase. The Forestry Commission's large areas must also be seen in the context of farming although these crops will not be harvested for up to 70 years after they are planted.

The mild climate of the south of the county made Tenby into a popular and fashionable resort during Georgian times and it fortunately retains much of its charm today. It was to Tenby that the first tourists to visit the area came some 130 years ago. The building of I.K. Brunel's broad gauge South Wales Railway in 1854 made the area that much more accessible although the great designer's plans were not prompted by tourism but by the trans-Atlantic liner trade which he hoped to attract to Neyland. Alas, this came to nothing but when the Great Western reached Fishguard in 1906 and the new harbour was opened, hopes were once more raised. However even that failed to attract the attention of the ship owners although the calling of the Cunard Line's greyhound *Mauretania,* on passage from New York to Liverpool, briefly raised local hopes. Today the port of Fishguard is the Sealink Stena Line terminal for Rosslare in the Republic of Ireland.

Another railway line worthy of mention is that linking Pembroke Dock and Tenby which was opened in 1863. At that time there was no connecting link, the line surviving in splendid isolation until it eventually joined up with the Great Western Railway at Whitland. There have been various moves to close it but thankfully it still survives as very much the epitome of the Welsh country

Part of the dramatic headland of St.Govan's Head. This area is a favourite spot for climbers to test their skills. (Nick Barnett)

railway. When some years ago, British Rail ran Inter City 125 trains on through services from Paddington to Pembroke Dock, where they linked with the B&I ferry service to Rosslare, their appearance on this slow and twisting branch line raised many a local eyebrow. Whoever would have imagined one of BR's fliers on so humble a railway?

In this brief essay, the surface of Pembrokeshire has been barely scratched. It is an ancient, wild and fascinating region – very much a land apart. Much has happened through the ages and it still changes today, attracting in excess of one million visitors each year. The presence of so many people is bound to have an effect on the county which now faces the challenge of how to absorb the tourists without changing the nature of its environment and the splendour of the wild areas which they come to visit. Car parks, litter bins, ice-cream vans, souvenir stalls, caravans and mobile homes are all part of late twentieth century Pembrokeshire. That it can cope, while retaining its essential remoteness, says much for the vast scale of the landscape which is still capable of passing on to the discerning visitor its unique blend of timelessness and solitude.

John Hendy

THE WILDSIDE OF PEMBROKESHIRE

"Once seen never forgotten" is a phrase that could sum up Pembrokeshire for many people. For in the spring and summer this far westerly county with its superb coastal scenery, islands, beaches, pleasant farmland and deep confiding lanes, is resplendent in a multi-coloured robe of flowers – there is a richness in wildlife habitat and diversity of species that is rarely matched in Britain.

Perhaps the most striking characteristics of the county are the A-shaped banks made of stone and earth, which shelter the traveller from the prevailing westerly winds.

These banks, together with thick hedgerows and sweeping verges are wildlife habitats in miniature. There are sheltered and exposed slopes, different soils, flashes of colourful brilliance and a correspondingly wide variety of species, which use this almost unique feature of the landscape. A coastal flavour pushes its way inland along the roadsides with drifts of white Scurvy Grass, Scentless Mayweed, pink patches of Thrift and pale blue Spring Squill to name but a few. Woodland species figure strongly too, Celandines, Primroses, Snowdrops, Bluebells, Wild Garlic and later Red Campion and the sentinels of the hedge banks, Foxgloves.

Trees, often leaning precariously away from the sea winds, can be of Ash or Oak but frequently Hazel and Sallow can be found in the damp more sheltered parts of the county. Blackthorn, Gorse, Sallow, Elder and Hazel bushes also punctuate these wildlife corridors that are used by voles, mice and Weasels, Slow-worms, Grass Snakes and lizards. Consequently, birds of prey like Kestrels hover over these rich food belts. Sparrowhawks and even Merlin can often be seen skirting the hedges, flying first one side then the other in a hope of surprising their prey. Buzzards use the height of the big trees to rest and watch out for prey and numerous and varied species of bats use the shelter of the hedgerows to feed on the insects that multiply in these tangled ribbons of life.

Dunnock and Yellowhammer, Robin and Blackbird, Lesser and Common Whitethroat are some of the birds of different habitats which breed in the hedges and still more use the food resources of berries and seeds which autumn brings. Look out for the special parts of these roadside areas, some are designated nature reserves in their own right for the rarer species.

Trees are scarce in much of Pembrokeshire, which is often windswept and exposed to salt spray. However, in the sheltered Nevern and Gwaun Valleys, and on the banks of the Daugleddau Estuary, there are pockets of ancient semi-natural woodlands. These areas are also rich in wildlife and history.

The sites that are worthy of note are found on the more sheltered and often inaccessible slopes, like Tycanol Woods. Set in a rabble of boulder scree and steep crags, short but old and gnarled sessile oaks grow in a luxuriance of lichen species that is exciting even to the uninformed observer. This is a woodland that has been grazed in the past, there is little regeneration nor vegetational ground cover. The light penetration to the ground is good providing ideal conditions for the rich variety of lichens to grow on the bark of the trees (the oaks have to be over a hundred years old to attract a cover of lichens). They hang "Greybeard" like from the branches, clinging to the trunks and spreading over the surface of the boulders under the trees and above on the crags. Over three hundred different lichen species can be found at this excellent site which in spring is carpeted in bluebells.

The Gwaun Valley (Cwmgwaun) east of Fishguard is a soothing place to visit. The trees here are tall and luxuriant, although even here the top trees are trimmed to the height of the valley by the wind. It is an area of mixed woodland, used originally for charcoal production: oaks (younger than at Tycanol), tall Ashes and old coppiced Hazel with its attendant textural cover of lichens, are just some of the woody species. The peace here away from the battering exposure of the coast is blissful with just the "hushing" of leaves in the

Wild Flowers of Pembrokeshire

1. *Profusion of spring flowers on the coastal path.*
2. *Western Gorse on Lydstep Head.*
3. *Thrift on the top of a typical earth and stone wall on Ramsey.*
4. *Thrift growing at the top of the rocky shore. (Photos: Anna Sutcliffe)*

1. A crop of wild carrot on the coast path.
2. A bank of Foxgloves on Skomer.
3. Gorse, heath and ling carpet on Lydstep Head.
4. Late spring bluebells around the farmhouse on Skomer.
(Photos: Anna Sutcliffe)

canopy above. Pied Flycatchers, Goldcrests, Blackcaps, Redstarts, Garden and Wood Warblers are summer residents. Buzzards are often to be seen soaring overhead. There is a timeless feeling about a walk in this place. Many of the paths are ancient roadways like that from Tregynon Farmhouse (an excellent place to stay) down into the valley. Views between the leaning tree trunks look down onto the wet meadows where horses graze. Ancient hazel coppice provide places for the Dormouse and there are a few records of the Harvest Mouse here too; Badgers are active, as are Foxes and Polecats. Visits to this valley, particularly from early spring reveal flowers in profusion, drifts of snowdrops, then bluebells and garlic. This is a really exciting and accessible place, which is enjoyable even from a car.

Pengelli Forest is now a nature reserve run by the Dyfed Wildlife Trust. It is a mixed woodland site of ancient origin which has been tampered with over the centuries. Some of the wood was used for charcoal and much of the bigger timber was used for pit props in the Welsh coal mines. The re-introduction of woodland management into Pengelli Forest by the Dyfed Wildlife Trust is injecting new life into this already superb site, nevertheless this is a site with a good deal of natural variety, which with the help of the Trust, is steadily improving. Sun dappled glades and rides that cut through the wood are patrolled by the Speckled Wood butterflies. Some of the more unusual species of butterflies are the Pearl Bordered and Silver Washed Fritillaries and the White Letter Hairstreak which feeds on the Wych Elm in a small part of the reserve. This is the only Welsh site for the Midland Hawthorn and uncommon plants include the Adders Tongue Fern, Wood Violet, Wood Millet and Wood Ruff.

The banks of the main river-estuary system, the Cleddau and its eastern and western arms are, in places, clothed in trees and there are some interesting semi-natural woodland species associated with them. The rare member of the Whitebeam family, the Wild Service Tree positively glows amongst the sessile oaks in the autumn, its golden red leaves with flashing white undersides and brilliant scarlet berries shouting for attention.

The roots of the trees extend almost down to the high tide level. There is little accessible foreshore to tempt people to land from boats but there are numerous small patches of reed bed, marsh and scrub up the fingers of the river which provide ideal habitat for the Otter. Indeed, the Western Cleddau has one of the highest densities of this beautiful shy animal in the whole of southern Britain.

The main estuary system runs out to sea between the headland of St Ann's and the Angle peninsula some fifteen miles from its tidal reach at Haverfordwest and Blackpool Mill. There are numerous inlets and bays of varying sizes although the principal shoreline is rocky – broad mudflats and saltmarshes are scarce.

Some sections of the estuary complex are important for wading birds and wildfowl. Near the seaward end the Gann estuary with its tidal pools, particularly the Pickleridge Pool behind the shingle bank and the saltmarsh must have something special as this area consistently turns up unusual birds. Spoonbills have overwintered here (and at Angle) in recent years, more transient rarities include Ruddy Shelduck, Little Egret, Red-necked Grebe and Baird's Sandpiper. The scrubby upperparts of the marsh host flocks of finches feeding on the seeds along the high tide line; Snipe and Woodcock rest up here after their night time feeding bouts in the fields.

The Gann saltmarsh with its thin, long-pile carpet of spotted colour is beautiful in its own way. Thrift, Sea Pink, Sea Lavender, Sea Aster, Sea Purslane, Glasswort, Sea Plantain, Scurvy grass, all typical of this habitat flower from spring onwards. Brown, distinctive smelling mud channels and glossy green banks of Sea Fescue, Scentless Mayweed and Sea Beet criss-cross this flat area. This is one of the more extensive pieces of salt marsh in Pembrokeshire.

On the southern shores the large, shallow Angle or

Kilpaison Bay (depending on which map you are using) attracts good numbers of wintering birds. In recent years this area has become less muddy and therefore not as productive for wading birds like Dunlin and Redshank. There is a bed of Narrow-leaved Eelgrass here which is good feeding for ducks like Wigeon. Just around the corner on the muddy shores of Pembroke River, there are often large flocks of Wigeon, Dunlin and Shelduck through the winter. The latter breed in small numbers in the summer.

The estuary as a whole is nationally important for its Redshank and Curlew and internationally important in cold weather for Shelduck and Teal, when total numbers of birds using the shelter and feeding can climb to over 20,000 birds. Some areas of the estuary are better than others, observe the low tide mudflats at Carew-Cresswell river junction and where the Western Cleddau separates from the Eastern Cleddau near Landshipping. The western arm from here is a winter wildfowl refuge as far as Haverfordwest. The upper end of the eastern arm hosts a Heronry towards Slebech and above Blackpool Mill there are Dippers and Kingfishers.

At Slebech, Pembroke Millpond and further down the estuary at Rhoscrowther and Angle for example, there are reed beds which provide important, if small areas, for birds and other animals to feed, breed and rest. The two latter mentioned sites are relatively undisturbed now, perhaps because of their close setting of the refineries and power station. The Cetti's Warbler has bred here since 1983, this now being the most westerly site for this little bird which has its breeding stronghold in the Mediterranean.

Coastal marshes and fens are few and far between (although they are generally larger in extent). Goodwick, in the north of the county, was formed years ago when the road and rail links were built across seafront, restricting the outflow of freshwater into the bay at Fishguard. Boardwalks allow entry into areas of tall reed bed; the swish and sway of the tall thin stems is an experience in itself but there is additionally the beautiful golden Kingcup to see in flower in the spring and a little later the Bog Myrtle.

Marloes Mere is a fen on the peninsula of that name. It is a small area of extreme richness botanically with Lesser Water Parsnip, Marsh Helleborine, Slender and Long Stalked Yellow Sedge, Fen Pondweed and Black Bogbean to name just a few species. There is no public access to this site although you can look over it easily from the track by the Marloes Youth Hostel and from Marloes car park. At the time of writing, in April 1991, it is anticipated that a hide will soon be erected here for birdwatchers. This site, particularly in winter, can be excellent. There are always good numbers of Teal and Mallard but it is the numbers of Shoveler which make the Mere so important. Other species of duck occur in small numbers and occasionally wild geese and swan are seen here. Hen Harriers are regular visitors in the winter and Peregrine Falcon often dash across the water trying to surprise Teal into the air; it is a good site for small birds too, particularly along the reed filled scrubby margins of the lane which meanders westwards from the car park towards Gateholm.

Dowrog Common, a few kilometres north-east of St. David's is a superb site of great diversity. It is owned by the National Trust and managed by the Dyfed Wildlife Trust, who, with much voluntary help, have helped to maintain and improve the site. Nearly 300 different plants have been identified in habitats ranging from wet and dry lowland, oceanic heath, grassland heath, tussock sedge fen, willow carr, valley marsh to open water. The setting is on common land where grazing has restricted tree growth, the shallow pools are edged with Pillwort and the floating white flowers of Water Plantain. A rich variety of dragon and damsel flies use this site in the summer but in winter Whooper and Bewick's Swans occasionally use the pools. Hen Harrier and Short-eared Owls are regular winter visitors suggesting that the small mammals and reptiles are numerous.

The largest area of freshwater in the county is in the flooded valley of Llys-y-fran. It is 78 hectares in extent

1. A cluster of sociable Puffins on Skomer.
2. Adult Cormorants on St. Margaret's Island, off Tenby.
3. Lesser Black-backed Gull on lichen encrusted rocks, Caldey. (Photos: Anna Sutcliffe)

A plump Manx Shearwater chick on Skomer

The "Solan goose" or Gannet among the rocks.

Short-eared Owl in the Bluebells of North Valley, Skomer. (Photos: Anna Sutcliffe)

but as it was only formed in 1971 the plant and animal life has not had time to diversify and enrich the waters. However, there are good numbers of Pochard, Tufted Duck and Lesser Black-backed Gulls using the water in the winter.

Bosherston Pools in the south of the county, is a very unusual lake and valley complex, originally designed by Capability Brown. The most spectacular flowers are the Water Lilies on the lake surface but much of the water vegetation is very rich and varied, thus encouraging a good deal of wildlife to feed and multiply here. One part of the lake is particularly good for a rare species of Stonewort, a type of calcareous alga.

The water birds that breed here include Coot, Moorhen, Mute Swan and the irridescent Kingfisher which patrols the lake edges. The winter brings in more Coot, sometimes several hundred, and flocks of Teal, Pochard, Mallard and Tufted Duck. Some of the more unexpected visitors have included Red Breasted Merganser, Night Heron, Ring Necked Duck and a Lesser Yellow Legs, blown well off course from its autumn passage.

Not only is this accessible site exciting for its variety, with Goldcrests and Firecrests calling at the very tops of the trees but there are also wintering roosts of finches, tits and warblers but it is also accessible. There are footpaths along two of the three arms and the system continues into tall trees near the site of the old Stackpole Court. All the appropriately marked paths are wide and good enough for access by wheelchair.

The seaward side of the pools is marked by Broad Haven beach. The beaches of Pembrokeshire are many and varied but are not distinguished for their wildlife; there are boulder beaches, shingle beaches with ridges and sand dunes in increasing value for wildlife along the coast.

The Pembrokeshire Coast National Park Authority is working hard to conserve and enhance some of the eroding sand dune systems with projects at several sites, including Freshwater East which was suffering badly

from the joint effects of many feet, wind and the sea. The golden mounds of Freshwater West and their setting between stark rocky headlands and behind a wild surf beaten beach make them special but there are other dune systems at Tenby, Barafundle, Broad Haven in the South of the County, Brownslade Burrows, Newport and on Caldey too. Sand dunes are fragile environments. In Pembrokeshire the yellow dune, often consists of Marram Grass and a few other species which hold the dunes in place but behind, on what is called the grey dune, the scented turf is a picture in the summer. Thyme and clover, sedges and pink Common Centaury and good stands of Pyramidal Orchid are some of the delights of these places. Other gems for the dunes of this old county include the attractive Sea Holly and Dune Gentian but many systems are badly eroded and blown out and Sea Buckthorn, originally planted to 'fix' the sand, has invaded some of them making them antisocial for both man and most other beasts.

The windblown sand on top of the cliffs provides ideal conditions for species like the Viper's Bugloss, which can be found in abundance near Barafundle.

All along the rocky cliffline there are bands or mottling of different coloured lichens, black near the sea, yellows further up in the splash zone and above this the pale grey-greens of the more diverse lichen communities merging near the top of the cliffs with the crevice growing plants. The extent of the banding is dependent on how exposed the rock face is to the high winds and big waves. Nationally important lichen assemblages are found at Manorbier, St. David's and Strumble Heads.

There is also a sequence of vegetation controlled by exposure to strong salt-laden winds, starting with a scattering of crevice plants and developing into coastal grassland, thence to taller coastal heath and then scrub with the ubiquitous Bracken. The cliff tops blush pink in late spring with the profusion of Thrift, in places the powder blue Spring Squill dominates with mounds of Sea Campion, more sheltered slopes can be thick with

Bosherston Lily Ponds. (South Pembrokeshire District Council)

Ox Eye Daisies. A close examination of grazed turf reveals tiny stunted versions of plants that you would otherwise recognise immediately, like Storksbill, Sorrel and Buckshorn Plantain. This often breathtaking display of flowers along almost all of the coast is best exemplified on St. David's Head where Kidney Vetch adds to the variety. Across the slopes of Strumble Headland there are Cowslips which mingle with Early Purple Orchids. On the damper, north facing slopes and where the soils are deeper, bluebells predominate using the bracken to shade the dying leaves later in the season.

The yellow and purple of Western Gorse and Heather is continued into the late summer and autumn when the maritime heath blooms. The north of the county has particularly fine displays of these species.

Any grazed turf near the coast is potentially good for the Chough. A walk along the coast is often enhanced by their joyful calls as they seemingly play with the air currents or exuberantly attack mounds of Thrift to dig out insects. The ponies and sheep on the Deer Park at Marloes are grazing the turf back to a condition which will benefit these excellent glossy black members of the Crow family with their scarlet beaks and matching coloured legs.

Peregrine Falcon and Ravens, Stonechat, Meadow and Rock Pipits, cave nesting House Martins and Swallows, can all be seen along the coastal fringes. Butterflies are another group commonly found here, Small Blues, Painted Ladies, Meadow and Hedge Browns, Graylings and Red Admirals are all well represented. Perhaps the most exciting insects are the Great Green Bush Cricket and the Glow-worm both of which are found on the Marloes Peninsula and along the coast.

Of all the counties in southern England and Wales this western coast has the best seabird colonies. There are some special places like the Elegug Stacks near Bosherston, where Guillemots crowd together on top of the rock columns just a few yards from the observer and Kittiwakes call noisily from the air to their compatriots on nests below. The Tree Mallow and Sea Beet, which grows in such luxuriance on these stacks is fertilised by the seabirds' guano. Nearby there is the Witches Cauldron, where Razorbills fly through a natural arch to circle upwards and around the great bowl to get to their breeding ledges.

The Kingfisher. (Anna Sutcliffe)

Good examples of other mainland colonies can be seen at Stackpole Head, Needle Rock and Dinas Island and there are scatterings of Herring Gulls and Fulmars all around the coast with a few colonies of Cormorants too. A few pairs of Great Black-backed Gulls claim a mainland territory nearly always fairly near to other seabirds so that dinner is readily at "beak."

A seabird spectacular can be experienced at Strumble Head during times of strong north westerly winds, especially in the months August to November. Thousands of birds stream past the cliffs, and rarities include; Sabine's Gull, Cory's Shearwater and Long Tailed Skua and many hundreds of Manx Shearwaters, gannets, auks and gulls can pass in one day.

Look out to sea from the main headlands and you should not be disappointed for there are often birds feeding or flying past, frequently schools of porpoise, dolphin and rarely turtles and sunfish are seen from these spectacular viewpoints.

The prize for the richest variety and the largest numbers of seabirds and the best acreage of flowers must go to the islands. Each one is special in its own way and all are worth that extra effort to go and see.

Starting in the north, there is Ramsey. Across Ramsey Sound, the island appears to be a patchwork of fields in the north east and the south is clothed in coastal heathland. This area gives a truly glowing display of purple heathers in August, the multitude of little flowers seem to hum with the weight of bees actively gathering pollen in the warm sun. The most striking features are the hills called Carn Ysgubor (whose slopes are covered in gorse scrub and topped by heather) and the highest peak at 136 metres of Carn Llundain to the south. These hills drop steeply down to the high cliffs of the western coast, where the seabirds breed on broad limestone ledges. The thin soils of the western and southern coasts, including the islets of Ynys Cantwr and Ynys Beri grow a beautiful carpet of late spring flowers. The squill is the dominant species to the extent that Ynys Beri can look as though a giant has sprinkled pale blue talcum powder on the slopes. Thrift and Sea Campion mix intimately in the cliff top turf.

The fields of grass in the north are grazed by a flock of sheep and a small herd of Red Deer. This turf must be excellent for invertebrates as Ramsey supports a good population of Chough, usually between 4 and 7 pairs, and one of the highest breeding densities of Lapwings in the whole of west Wales, numbering about thirty pairs in all. However, the island has few other ground nesting birds as the predators, rats and feral cats, effectively prevent Puffins, Manx Shearwaters or Short-eared Owls returning to breed here.

The inaccessible, ungrazed sections of the east coast of this island are luxuriant in a wonderfully rich mix of coastal heath and scrub vegetation. Here a prostrate form of Juniper grows, a species from a relict heath of centuries ago. There is also royal fern, sloe, garlic, tangles of Honyesuckle and Ivy and wet flushes of some interesting water plants. The farm guesthouse and buildings snuggle into the largest valley with the only big stream of the island. In this area there are some interesting species like Fiddle Dock to look out for.

This is a rich island, which has much more to be discovered. It is best known for the Grey Seals that breed in the caves, coves and on the beaches around the island. About 350 pups are born here each year, making this the largest Grey Seal nursery in southern Britain.

From the hill tops of Ramsey, the views are unsullied all the way round the compass, from Whitesand Bay and the blue black mountain of Carn Llidi and the other Presely hills northwards, round to the lower coastal cliffs in the horseshoe of St Bride's Bay in the east. Swing to the west and there are the Bishops and Clerks with the South Bishop lighthouse blinking day and night, warning shipping of the treacherous reefs. On the horizon is a bun shaped rock which if you look closer has a white capping on one side, this bleached section is a large colony of nesting Gannets and their white guano.

Grassholm is the second largest gannetry in the Atlantic. To visit is the ultimate sight, sound and smell experience of the the Pembrokeshire coast. There are possibly over 30,000 pairs of these bulky birds nesting on their stick and flotsam built nests all covered in a whitewash of droppings. Perhaps, the main reasons why the island is such a success as far as the gannets are concerned is that these "solan geese", as they were known, with a wing span of two metres, need air space to take off. This hard lump of intrusive igneous rock which rises high out of the water is ideal for the birds to gain lift into the prevailing winds. Such large birds also need lots of food and the richness of the fishing in the Smalls grounds just a few wingbeats from the colony is undoubtedly a large bonus.

Gannets are around the colony from February until October. Early in the season the golden yellow wash on the head and neck as well as their coloured markings on the eyes and the toes of the black feet are brightly coloured, being used in their courtship displays. The single egg hatches in mid-June and the chicks are then fed on a rich diet of regurgitated fish. Development takes them from fluffy white chicks to very fat things that moult their fluff all over the little island so that even the collapsed puffin burrows and the cappings of grass on the opposite side to the main colony is white in drifts of feathers. By the time the adults leave, the fledglings are speckled black and glossy. They are also heavier than their parents as they now have an intensive period of learning without parental guidance, so "do-it-or-die"

A woodland scene in the spring in Pembrokeshire (South Pembrokeshire District Council)

Warden's House on Skomer. (Anna Sutcliffe)
Inset: A dramatic view from Skomer head, as the Dale Princess *makes her way around the island from the mainland. (John Hendy)*

is their motto. They have to leave the nest, swim out to sea, learn to fly and also get the hang of plunge diving for fish. This spectacular method of diving is marvellous to watch but is extremely risky for the birds, one false entry and a dislocated wing or more instantly a broken neck spell the end of many a gannet in the first year of life.

An evening trip from Martin's Haven around Skomer, or to Grassholm, can also give you good views of porpoise and dolphin from the boat. Rafts of Manx Shearwaters amass off Skomer and Skokholm in the evenings waiting for the protection of nightfall before they fly into their burrows on the islands. There can also be fleeting glimpses of Storm Petrels and gannets feeding, around this coast. Skomer and Skokholm are now a "Special Protection Area" designated in 1983 under an EEC convention for the protection of the breeding seabirds.

Skomer is the largest island in the group at 294 hectares and has perhaps the richest diversity of birds and animals of all the islands. It is primarily a seabird reserve, owned by the Countryside Commission for Wales and managed by the Dyfed Wildlife Trust.

One of the smaller mammals on this island is the unique Skomer Vole, which has evolved into a separate island race of the Bank Vole. It is larger, has a more rufous coloured coat and is comparatively tame to handle as Skomer has only aerial predators and the best way to escape these is to freeze when danger is near. It has a diet of bracken, interesting because this plant contains carcinogenic chemicals which seem not to affect the Skomer Vole. The Pygmy and Common Shrew, Wood Mouse and Rabbit, introduced as a cash crop in the 1300's and now numbering well over 8.000 animals, are the other island mammals.

The only evidence of the 165,000 pairs of shearwaters on the island in the daytime are the remains of Ravens' and Great Black-backed Gulls' dinner or the strange grating calls in the burrows deep underground.

It is the large numbers of holes all over the island which strike you on the first visit to Skomer. These are the entrances to the homes of rabbits, shearwaters and on the edges of the cliffs puffins as well as a few small colonies of Jackdaws. Climbing the purpose built steps is the toughest part of getting to Skomer but once at the top the rest is gently undulating hills or level ground. Grey rocky ridges covered with lichens cross the island from west to east and these are two main wet areas in the North and South valleys, providing cover for migrants in the sallow bushes, tall vegetation and reeds that grow there.

The highest point is at the farm in the middle of the island at 78 metres. This elevated point gives an overview of the island's surface showing the close grazed turf of the central cultivated, fields where seed corn and potatoes have been grown in the past. The derelict, slate-fronted farmhouse, with its remains of a patio on the front, is of a size which suggests that the owners in the hey day of farming here were rich. They had shooting parties and the descendents of the Pheasants that survived can be seen today. It is a breathtaking place to visit, two thirds of the island can be covered in the blue, reds, white and pink hues of the flowers that thrive here, although in the last few years the hot dry summers and winter storms have wrought havoc on the more exposed headlands and dry slopes.

The most interesting birds to be seen on the one tree top of the island are the Short-eared Owls in the heather and the Pintail at North Pond. (The first breeding record for Wales). Besides these, Lapwing, Curlew and Oystercatchers use the island and the Lesser Black-back Gulls raucously rule their colony areas.

The edge of the island is mainly precipitous cliff with the main seabird colonies on the south coast and on the cooler north and east facing rocky ledges. Perhaps a third of a million birds use this island to bring up their annual crop of chicks. It is a fast and furious season with the last birds to arrive being the Puffins and Shearwaters in the month of March. The first to leave are the Guillemots and Razorbills in mid-July with the Puffins and Kittiwakes close on their heels by the start of August. Shearwaters and Fulmars leave by September and the latter are the first to return again in November.

The waters around the island were made into Britain's' second marine reserve in early July 1990. The richness of species found above the tideline is continued below into the murky depths and for 1,500 hectares around Skomer and the coastline nearby. Here are some of the fastest running tidal races in Britain. Almost every conceivable habitat can be found in the waters around the island, from the extremes of shelter and exposure, shallow to deep water, slopes of different angles – flat beds to precipitous cliffs, different substrates from loose mud and sand to rock, smooth or rough surfaces. Each parameter and combination of conditions being crucial for the different species that are found on the reserve. In North Haven there is bed of Zostera marina, a type of eelgrass which in the 1930's was virtually wiped out due possibly to a virus. Skomer's eelgrass is one of a very few populations that escaped. There are such things as soft corals called Red Sea Fingers, Gold and Scarlet Star Corals in the most northern part of their distribution and beautiful Sea Fans, some of which are over 80 centimetres tall and have an estimated age of a hundred years.

Just to the east of Skomer is Middleholm, a small island whose rocky shores are swept by both Little and Jack Sounds. There is a colony of Shag on this island which is locally important.

Skokholm lies three kilometres south of Skomer and a similar distance west from the Marloes peninsula. The island has been owned by the Dale Castle Estate since the mid eighteenth century and is managed by the Dyfed Wildlife Trust. Of all the islands Skokholm is the most welcoming and instantly attractive. The geology is of warm coloured Old Red Sandstone with the variable hues showing layers which are now moulded into waves and peaks, cut into teeth-like blocks and generally providing a pleasing impression on all who visit. To the east, the cliffs are about 20m high but they rise to 50m in the west, and are capped by an icing white lighthouse with a boulder quarry beneath. This quarry is occupied by a large colony of Storm Petrels – the biggest colony in the Irish Sea.

It was Ronald Lockley who started Britain's first Bird Observatory here in 1933. The ringing ceased in 1976 but detailed records are kept every day of all the birds seen on and around the island. Being so far offshore common birds can be rare, such as House Sparrow, Bullfinch, any of the Tits and even Magpie, a species which breeds on Skomer. In contrast rare birds are often recorded and the first British records of Bonelli's and Olivaceous Warblers and the Swainson's Thrush were from Skokholm.

The flowers are superb, not just the profusion of the small purple heads of Violets and Ground Ivy mixed with shiny yellow Celandine and the paler Primroses in south valley but the Heartsease on the slope of Crab Bay. There are exuberant displays of the Sea Campion, Thrift and Scentless Mayweed along the north and west coasts.

Caldey is the third largest island at 255 hectares. As far as the natural history is concerned it is quite different from the other islands in a lot of ways, there are no seabird colonies of note. A large section of the island is planted with trees in the only sheltered valley and the slopes behind the golden beach of Priory Bay are covered in windblown sand forming some floristically rich sand dunes and dune slack. One of the ponds has several plants of the rare Greater Spearwort growing in it. Although there is an excellent variety of plants found here, the native vertebrates are very poorly represented. There are no toads, slow worms or newts and rabbits were removed in 1975. There is only the Brown Rat which thrives, and the recently introduced frogs and hedgehogs.

Birds that are rarely seen on the other islands breed here, Treecreepers, Blackcaps, Mistle Thrush, Greenfinch, Yellowhammer, Blue and Great Tits. Shelduck are thought to breed but besides these, Caldey

Sandtop Bay, Caldey. This view from Caldey takes in St. Margaret's Island and Lydstep point. (Anna Sutcliffe)

Above: Young Grey seal pup. (Anna Sutcliffe)
Right: Young rabbit – introduced to the islands as a cash crop in the 14th century. (Anna Sutcliffe)

nowadays has a poor selection of seabirds. In the 1970's the largest colony of Herring Gulls was to be found along the coast but in recent years this population, which peaked at three and a half thousand pairs, has fallen to seven hundred pairs.

St Margaret's Island is joined to Caldey at low water by a reef of rocks. On this small island with its steep cliffs and old quarries there are a selection of seabirds and the largest colony of Cormorants in Wales, numbering about three hundred pairs.

The Presely Hills, standing at a maximum of 541 metres above sea level, are like islands above the Pembrokeshire I have described. Rocky tors thrust above the sheep grazed, grey green upland grasses and heather moorland. There are peaty hollows, damp depressions where bog plants thrive. Here is the Welsh stronghold of the Western Clubmoss; sundew, butterworts and sphagnum mosses may be found here too. This is a wild and breathless place and on a clear day Pembrokeshire can be seen in its entirety. All the pieces of the puzzle of this excitingly varied county are before you. Look out the pale turquoise sea and you will see dark shadows of clouds scudding landward over the sands, up the cliffs, melting its shape to the soft hues of the landscape.

Anna Sutcliffe.

PEMBROKESHIRE COAST NATIONAL PARK

The Pembrokeshire Coast National Park is one of eleven National Parks in England and Wales. The Park was officially designated on 29th February 1952 under the provisions of the National Parks and Access to the Countryside Act 1949, and is one of the smallest of the Parks. It is also unique in that it is the only National Park in Britain which is largely coastal and which for the most part covers lowland areas. It is also fairly densely populated, and 80% of it is actively farmed. It covers an area of 225 square miles, with richly varied coastal scenery, offshore islands, the quiet and secluded stretches of the Milford Haven Waterway, and the moorlands of the Presely Hills.

The eleven National Parks of England and Wales contain the most beautiful, spectacular and dramatic areas of countryside. They cover nearly ten per cent of the land, but the areas included are in no sense nationally owned. Although a national park may contain stretches of common land, and there may also be pockets of the landscape owned by or managed by the Park Authority, or by bodies such as the National Trust, the Forestry Commission, the Countryside Council for Wales and other conservation groups, most of the land is still in private ownership.

The National Parks were created in the early Fifties as a result of public pressure in the '30s and '40s to encourage access and enjoyment, and to protect areas of countryside which were regarded as the most beautiful in England and Wales; these areas are also rich in wildlife, and in historical and geological associations. The chief aim of the National Parks is to conserve the landscape including the distinctive ways of life found within them, whilst providing opportunities for quiet enjoyment and recreation.

In order to carry out these aims, a National Park Committee was created; it has its own staff, and is a Committee of Dyfed County Council. Of the monies needed for the funding of the National Park, 75% is received from national Government via the Countryside Council for Wales and 25% is received from the local councils, although with other grants (and income generation) the local charge payer only contributes about 5% of total expenditure.

The National Park Committee consists of 18 members; 10 are Dyfed County Councillors, appointed by the County, two other members are appointed by Preseli Pembrokeshire and South Pembrokeshire District Councils respectively. A further six members are appointed by the Secretary of State for Wales. This blend of members is intended to reflect and balance those competing national and local interests which affect the National Park.

The Committee is assisted by the full-time National Park Officer and the staff of the National Park Department. This Department consists of four main elements, Planning, Information, Rangers, Management, all of which are assisted by a secretariat.

Planning Services consists of two sectors. The first of these is Forward Planning which deals with long-term planning issues, conducting surveys and research for a variety of purposes, including planning, ecological studies and experimental management schemes. This section also works closely with the farming community, through its Agricultural Liaison Officer.

Development Control deals with planning permission for new housing and other forms of development within the Park, and the planning enforcement section deals with the question of unauthorised development.

The Ranger Service are the main contact with the public in the field. There are 3 teams of 2 full-time Rangers, one team for each sector of the Park. They patrol the park at all times of the year and especially in summer to encourage considerate behaviour in the interests of farmers. They keep in touch with local residents, especially in the countryside, assist the public, deal with emergencies, maintain liaison with Police, Coastguard and other services, assist with organised

The quiet and pleasant setting of Little Haven (Pembrokeshire Eye)

The North Beach, Tenby and Goscar Rock. (South Pembrokeshire District Council)

recreation events within the Park and carry out practical management tasks. Each Ranger has a special interest such as nature conservation and assists with surveys, leads guided walks and talks, and organises the work of Voluntary Wardens in his sector. The 80 unpaid Voluntary Wardens help in their own free time with maintenance work and surveys, leading Walks and manning information points at local events.

The Authority administers seven Information Centres at Newport, St. David's, Broad Haven, Pembroke, Tenby, Kilgetty and Saundersfoot for the benefit of residents and visitors. The Centres attract about 320,000 people annually and the Information Section organises an extensive Interpretation programme including exhibitions and more than 300 activities and events each year to improve public awareness of the local environment. The Park Authority also produces publications, sells a wide range of books on subjects related to the National Park and conservation, and maintains liaison with educational organisations and the Wales Tourist Board.

The Park Authority owns or leases about 1000 acres of land including buildings, car parks, boat parks, picnic areas and woodland. Almost all the foreshore of the coast and estuaries in the National Park is also leased by the Authority from the Crown Commissioners. These holdings are administered and maintained by Management Services Section.

This section also gives technical advice on woodland management, and landscaping, assists with voluntary conservation projects, plans new facilities, conducts land acquisition and carries out construction work. The Authority maintains the 167 mile Pembrokeshire Coast Path, with grant aid from the Countryside Council for Wales, as well as another 450 miles of link and inland paths.

At present the authority is directed by Mr Nic Wheeler, the National Park Officer. It has around 65 full-time staff and about 36 seasonal staff are employed each summer on maintenance work, in Information

Llawhaden Castle. (Miles Cowsill)

Centres, as temporary wardens and car park attendants.

Pressures on the Park are not likely to diminish; planning applications (for example) continue to flow in at over 800 per year – the vast majority of these are approved but there must be constant vigilance to protect the fragile character of the landscape. Specialised habitats, like the coastal margins and the Daugleddau Estuary, must be monitored to determine whether new management regimes need to be introduced.

The built environment contains much that is special, such as the Georgian terraces of Tenby and the Palmerston forts around the Haven. The National Park Authority will seek to protect these – and help local communities to assess community needs (such as housing) with a view to helping other bodies maintain viable residential settlements within the Park area.

There is also the challenge of persuading central Government of the vital need for substantial increases in funding for essential works – and the increasingly important role of the volunteers in many aspects of the Park's work.

SOUTH PEMBROKESHIRE

The District of South Pembrokeshire is situated in the south-west of Wales and is known as "Little England Beyond Wales". South Pembrokeshire is quite small, totalling only 440 square kilometres, but within this area there can be found an impressive range of landscapes, history and wildlife.

The region is one of great diversity. To the north, Narberth is a small rural market town servicing the lower reaches of the Presely Hills. In the east are the resorts of Tenby and Saundersfoot, set in spectacular coastal scenery, they have gained an international reputation. In the west, Pembroke and Pembroke Dock lie on the southern banks of the Milford Haven Waterway.

Today Tenby is one of the most popular holiday resorts in Wales and boasts a wealth of narrow streets, houses and shops built against the ruins of the 13th century town walls. The main part of the town is set on a rocky promontory, overlooking two magnificent sandy bays.

Tenby became a popular health resort in the 18th century and, on the coming of the railway in 1853, the town developed into a major holiday resort. Most holiday makers today travel to Tenby in buses and cars from all over the British Isles and the World. The traditional tourist markets of the West Midlands and the North West of England are still important to the town but in recent years the South-East of England market has shown considerable growth. Many of the large Georgian buildings, which were used as second family homes or hotels during the early part of this century, have been converted in the Eighties into flats to provide smaller holiday properties or retirement homes.

The pleasant village of Saundersfoot has developed as a popular location for yachting and for holiday-makers wanting to enjoy the the golden sands of Carmarthen Bay. The attractive little harbour, constructed in 1829 for the purpose of exporting locally mined coal, is now the home for many pleasure boats.

Pembroke is an important commercial and tourist centre. The main town is contained within the original walls. Modern developments have been built around the old town to house the influx of construction workers in the Sixties and Seventies for the Texaco Refinery and Pembroke Power Station.

Pembroke Dock is located about about 2 miles north of Pembroke town and stands on the Milford Haven Estuary. Until 1926 the town was one of the chief naval dockyards in Britain, boasting the building of the first Royal Yacht – *Victoria and Albert* in 1834 and the first ironclad warship *Warrior,* now restored and berthed at Portsmouth. During the Second World War the town was the base for the famous RAF Sunderland flying boats. Today, the town accommodates a daily ferry to Rosslare and a new deep-water harbour handling cargoes from all over the world.

The population of South Pembrokeshire is about 41,000. Tourism is reckoned to generate about £100 million turnover per annum. Agriculture continues to be a primary industry with its famous red potatoes. Dairy and arable farming predominate. During the mid-Eighties, unemployment figures were unacceptably high in the area, and this led to the designation of parts of Pembroke Dock as an Enterprise Zone to encourage industry to the district. Other areas of South Pembrokeshire have attracted special support from both the Welsh Development Agency and the Wales Tourist Board.

If the Celtic Sea is developed for oil in the future Pembroke Dock may well become a 'little Aberdeen' as the town offers probably some of the best port facilities in West Wales. Tourism will continue to expand into the next century, and the industry will continue to cater for the changing tourist market, as it has done in recent years with the development of Oakwood Park Leisure Centre, near Narberth.

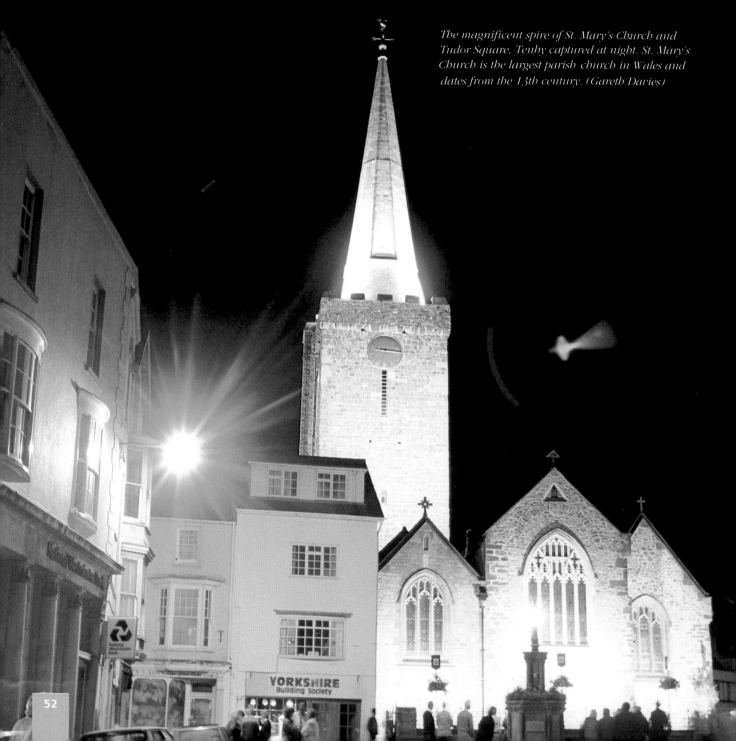

The magnificent spire of St. Mary's Church and Tudor Square, Tenby captured at night. St. Mary's Church is the largest parish church in Wales and dates from the 13th century. (Gareth Davies)

Top: The picturesque beach at Wisemans Bridge looking out to sea takes in Monkstone Point. The beach was named after the Wyseman family who owned extensive lands in the area. The beach was used in the Second World War as practice for the Normandy landings. (Miles Cowsill)

Left: The village of Amroth is situated near the old eastern boundary of the old counties of Pembrokeshire and Carmarthenshire. The village also marks the start of the 167 mile long Pembrokeshire Coast Path which leads as far as Poppit Sands, near St.Dogmaels in the north of the county. (Pembrokeshire Eye)

The mighty castle of Pembroke captured in the morning sun. The outer wall has seven bastion towers, and the keep is 75 feet high.
(Miles Cowsill)

A view from Saundersfoot harbour. (Miles Cowsill)

*Right: The serene and inviting clear waters of Skrinkle Beach.
(Pembrokeshire Eye)*

*Below: Manorbier Castle dates back to the 12th century and it
is thought to have been more of a baronial residence than a
fortress. The castle dominates the village and the attractive
sandy cove below. (South Pembrokeshire District Council)*

The beautiful and tranquil setting of Carew Castle on the banks of the Cleddau estuary. (South Pembrokeshire District Council)

1. The attractive village of St.Florence pictured in the spring. The village was until the mid 19th century on an inlet of the sea, which was in medieval times a harbour.

2. Carew Cheriton church captured in the late evening sunshine.

3. The 13th century cliffside chapel set into the rockface at St. Govan's Head. (Photos: Miles Cowsill)

1. *The village of Rhoscrowther shadowed by Texaco Refinery.*

2. *A typical lunchtime view for residents of Front Street, as the B&I ferry* Munster *arrives at Pembroke Dock on her daily sailing from Ireland.*

3. *A quiet street scene in Pembroke Dock.*
   (Photos: Miles Cowsill)

Stackpole Quay. (Pembrokeshire Eye)

Looking out from West Angle Bay towards
Thorn Island and Dale Roads.
(Miles Cowsill)

Right: The sweeping and wild bay of
Freshwater West looking towards Linney
Head. (Miles Cowsill)

Looking down the coast from St. Govan's Head towards Stackpole Head. Caldey Island can be seen in the far background. (South Pembrokeshire District Council)

Blackpool Mill. (Miles Cowsill)

NORTH PEMBROKESHIRE

The Preseli Pembrokeshire District Council covers more than two-thirds of the former county area. The population of North Pembrokeshire exceeds 70,000 and covers area of some 450 square miles. Like South Pembrokeshire, the north of the county has an impressive range of landscapes, history and wildlife. The major towns of the district have their special ingredients character and charm.

Haverfordwest was until 1974 the county town of Pembrokeshire, when the county was merged into Dyfed. The town has lost some of its commercial importance, nevertheless with its historical buildings, market and new shopping centre it still retains the feel of being a county town.

Milford Haven is situated on the steeply sloping ground on the north shores of the drowned valley of the Haven. The town dates back to the late 18th century, when it was developed as a naval dockyard and fishing port. The town developed as a deep-sea fishing port after naval operations moved to Pembroke Dock, the port at one time had the fourth biggest fishing catch in Britain. Today the importance of fishing has declined with only a handful of fishing vessels.

The city of St.David's is the most hallowed place in Wales as the birthplace of 6th century Dewi Sant (St.David), who grew up to become the patron saint of Wales. The city of St.David's is also the smallest cathedral city in Britain, with only a population of around 1,500. The city attracts many thousands of visitors each year from all over the world with its harmonious and pleasant setting.

Fishguard with its fine bay, is surrounded by steep cliffs and includes a large stone breakwater stretching ½ mile out to sea. The harbour, located at the little village of Goodwick, is served today by one of the most modern ferries on the Irish Sea. Prior to the harbour being built, the town was famous for herring fishing and pilchard curing.

Haverfordwest's new shopping centre is located next the river and was opened during 1990. (Miles Cowsill)

In the southern part the farmers work their land to produce the famous early potatoes. Dairy cattle and some arable farming can found also but as you move north sheep and upland farming becomes more important.

Tourism in North Pembrokeshire generates something in the region of £60 million a year. The district council have gone to great lengths in recent years to attract more visitors to North Pembrokeshire. The other main industries of Preseli Pembrokeshire are Oil Refining, Fishing and medium sized manufacturing. Part of the district has been designated as an Enterprise Zone to attract new business and employment.

Like South Pembrokeshire, the area is trying to meet the needs of the changing developments in tourism. The new Brunel Quay Marina at Neyland has been built in recent years and has attracted a wealth of boats from all over Europe. Other changes and improvements will continue to be made to meet the next decade of tourists.

In July 1991 Milford Haven Waterway is due to be graced by a wonderful display of sailing vessels at the start of the famous Cutty Sark Tall Ships Race. (FotoFlite)

Inset: The January sun captures the harbour of Milford Haven with two of Sealink's ferries Cambridge Ferry and Earl William laid-up for their winter spell at the port. The main town can be seen set up on the hill behind the once bustling fishing port. (Miles Cowsill)

Dale is one of the most popular sailing centres of the area, enjoying a sheltered position in the lee of the Dale Peninsula. (Pembrokeshire Eye)

Looking down Hill Lane, Haverfordwest towards the castle. (Miles Cowsill)

Hamilton Terrace, Milford Haven in the spring sun. (Miles Cowsill)

The extensive sands of Broad Haven looking north towards Black Point. (Miles Cowsill)

Originally Solva was a bustling port. Today it is a favourite holiday centre with its attractive cottages and charming inlet harbour. In 1773 Solva was the base for the assembly of one of the first Smalls lighthouses. (Pembrokeshire Eye)

The inlet harbour of Porth Clais. (Pembrokeshire Eye)

St. David's Cathedral. (Miles Cowsill)
Inset: Bishop's Palace, St. David's. (Miles Cowsill)

The nave of St.David's Cathedral. (Pembrokeshire Eye)

Right: Little girl in traditional Welsh costume. (Pembrokeshire Eye)

Whitesand is one of the most popular beaches of North Pembrokeshire, with its fine sands and excellent surfing. This view takes in the bay and the fine mountain of Carn Llidi which stands some 600 feet above the sea level. (Miles Cowsill)

Right: St.David's lifeboat station located at Porthstinan looking out towards Ramsey. Close to the lifeboat station is the historical St.Justinian's Chapel. Justinian founded the small religious community on Ramsey. (Miles Cowsill)

Below: The disused slate quarry flooded at Abereiddi known as the 'Blue Lagoon'. (Miles Cowsill)

The coastal hamlet of Abercastle (Miles Cowsill)

*Above: The little and picturesque harbour at Porthgain.
(Miles Cowsill)*

Left: One of the most dramatic New Stone-age cromlechau located just west of the village of Abercastle. The stones formed a burial chamber as a family grave for some of the first farmers of Europe around 3000 B.C. In the background of this scene, the wild and dramatic coast of Pembrokeshire can seen looking up to Strumble Head. (Miles Cowsill)

Above: Picturesque and sheltered Lower Fishguard captured in the last few minutes of the winter sun. Afon Gwaun from the Presely Mountains flows rapidly into the natural home for many of the town's boats. (Miles Cowsill)

Right: Carregwastad. French forces landed at this point in February 1797, the last time Britain was invaded by a foreign power. (Pembrokeshire Eye)

The quiet bay of Pwllgwaelod, situated to the west of Dinas Head. (Pembrokeshire Eye)

The Parish Church of St.Brynach, Nevern. (Miles Cousill)

Top: The remains of the
12th century St. Dogmael's
Abbey. (Miles Cowsill)

Left: The Parish Church of New Moat, which was almost rebuilt
in the 1870's, except for the tower. (Miles Cowsill)

Right: Eleventh-century High Cross at Nevern. (Miles Cowsill)

Two views taken high up in the Presely Mountains. The highest point of the mountain range is Foel-cwmcerwyn. (Miles Cowsill/Pembrokeshire Eye)

Newport Bay. (Pembrokeshire Eye)

Parish church at Llanrhian in the spring. (Miles Cowsill)

ACKNOWLEDGMENTS

I am grateful for the assistance of all those who have kindly contributed to this publication.

Firstly, I would like to thank Dillwyn Miles, Anna Sutcliffe and John Hendy for their valuable contributions to the publication and also for checking the proofs.

My thanks also go to Mr D. Jackson and Mr Paul Randall of National Power, Pembroke for agreeing to sponsor the publication and for providing the foreword to the book.

I wish to express gratitude to the following photographers for their assistance:–

John Evans, PO Box 5, Fishguard SA65 9BZ
Gareth Davies, 16a The Norton, Tenby. (0834 3357)
Brace Harvatt Associates, 5 Hill Street, Haverfordwest. (0437 765391)
FotoFlite, Littlestone Road, New Romney, Kent TN28 8LW. (0679 64891)
Pembrokeshire Eye, The Paddock, Port Lion, Llangwm. (0646 600754)

The following are also thanked for photographs and information:

Richard Howells and Norman Jenkins (Preseli Pembrokeshire District Council), Nic Wheeler and Stephen Drinkwater (Pembrokeshire Coast National Park), Ashley Warlow (Gulf Oil Refining Ltd.), Kefin Wakefield (South Pembrokeshire District Council), Phil Thompson (Texaco Ltd), Hugh and Maryann Foster, Ted Goddard, David Robinson, Gillian Richardson and Vincent West.

I would like to thank Ian Smith and Joy Sandifer of Bézier Design Ltd, Camrose House, Main Street, Pembroke, SA71 4HN. (Tel 0646 686418) for all their help with layout and design of the publication.

Finally I would like to express my gratitude to Roger Ferris, Managing Director, Andrew Lowe and all the staff of Haven Colourprint for their help and support with this publication.

● ●

BIBLIOGRAPHY

The Pembrokeshire Coast National Park ....Dillwyn Miles
Portrait of Pembrokeshire ....Dillwyn Miles
The Tourist Guide to the Pembrokeshire Islands ......Anna Sutcliffe
The Pembrokeshire Guide ....Brain John
Pembrokeshire Illustrated ....Brain John
The Pembrokeshire Explorer ....Roger Worsley
Fishguard – Rosslare ....Miles Cowsill

● ●

Inside back cover: *Sunrise over Fishguard Bay and Dinas Head. (John Evans)*

Back cover:

(Left) The rough seas of the Bristol Channel breaking onto the rocks at St.Govan's Head. (Miles Cowsill)

(Top right) Looking up Castle Terrace towards Pembroke Castle in the snow. (Miles Cowsill)

(Bottom right) The golden looking beach of Marloes Sands with Gateholm in the far distance. (Brace Harvatt Associates)

Look out for CARDIGANSHIRE in Profile

available in all good bookshops from spring 1992.

Price £4.95

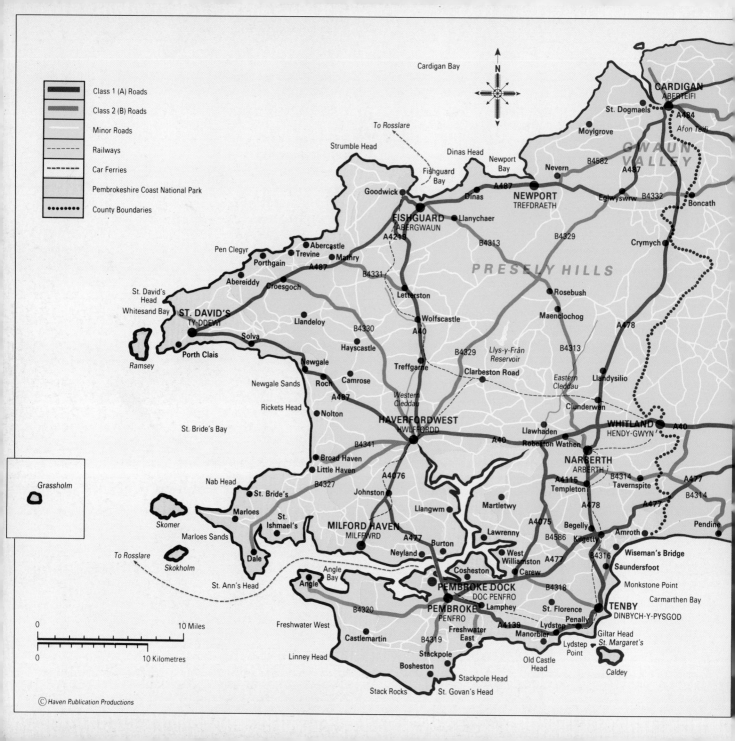